this book belong,

Kaylee Puffer
me from Monica given to
Christmas 2001

O9-BUD-598

Laura's Album

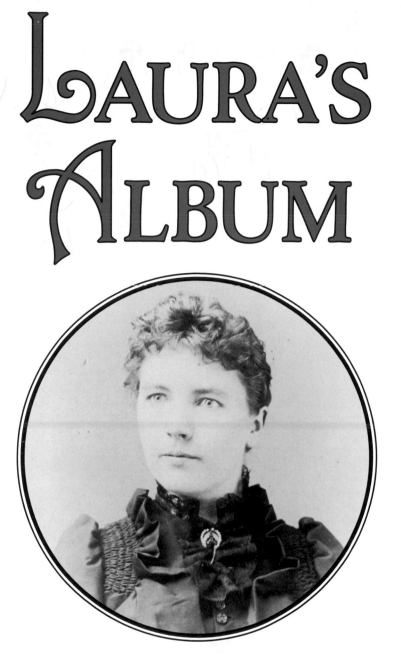

A REMEMBRANCE SCRAPBOOK OF

Laura Ingalls Wilder

COMPILED BY WILLIAM ANDERSON

HARPERCOLLINS*PUBLISHERS*

HarperCollins® and ♦® are registered trademarks of HarperCollins Publishers Inc.

Laura's Album
Copyright © 1998 by William Anderson
Illustrations copyrights: 1935, renewed 1963, by HarperCollins Publishers Inc. (p. 52, 57); 1937,
renewed 1965, by HarperCollins Publishers Inc. (p. 53, 58); 1932, renewed 1959, by HarperCollins Publishers Inc.
(p. 54–55); 1933, renewed 1961, by HarperCollins Publishers Inc. (p. 56); 1939, renewed 1967 by HarperCollins
Publishers Inc. (p. 59); 1941, renewed 1969, by HarperCollins Publishers Inc. (p. 65); 1953, renewed 1981, by Garth
Williams (p. 68–69, 72–73, 79), except for *The First Four Years*, 1971 by Garth Williams (p. 68).

All rights reserved. No part of this book may be used or reproduced in any manner whatsoever
without written permission except in the case of brief quotations embodied in critical articles and reviews.
Printed in Hong Kong. For information address HarperCollins Children's Books,
a division of HarperCollins Publishers, 1350 Avenue of the Americas, New York, NY 10019.
www.harperchildrens.com

Library of Congress Cataloging-in-Publication Data
Anderson, William, date
    Laura's album : a remembrance scrapbook of Laura Ingalls Wilder / compiled by William Anderson.
        p.   cm.
    Summary: Photographs and mementos accompany an account of the life and literary career of the author of the well-loved
"Little House" books.
    ISBN 0-06-027842-0
    1. Wilder, Laura Ingalls, 1867–1957—Biography—Juvenile literature.   2. Wilder, Laura Ingalls, 1867–1957—Biography—Pictorial
works.   3. Women authors, American—20th century—Biography—Juvenile literature.   4. Women authors, American—20th century—
Biography—Pictorial works.   5. Frontier and pioneer life—United States—Juvenile literature.   6. Frontier and pioneer life—United
States—Pictorial works.   [1. Wilder, Laura Ingalls, 1867–1957.   2. Women authors.   3. Authors.   4. Women—Biography.]   I. Title.
PS3545.I342Z5582   1998   97-49332
813'.52—dc21   CIP
[B]   AC
Designed by Alicia Mikles
5   6   7   8   9   10
❖

Title page: Laura Ingalls Wilder, around 1906. Opposite: Laura swinging on an Ozark grapevine.

CONTENTS

PROLOGUE

I am sure that Laura Ingalls Wilder would be amazed if she knew that forty years after her death in 1957, her Little House books, and indeed all of her extant writings, had become staples in homes, libraries, schools, and bookshops all over the world. Laura transformed her memories of her pioneer childhood into books that became classics in her own lifetime and won her national and worldwide admiration. But she always accepted praise and honors for her writing with hesitancy, preferring to pass along the respect that came her way to the pioneers who had moved west to the Great Plains and forests where she had grown up. The audience for Laura's stories continues to expand as each new generation discovers the Little House books. Readers—often introduced to these books by their parents, who first read them when they themselves were children—pass these books on to *their* children, and families are inspired by the Little House stories to remember and share their own pasts.

Laura (left) and Rose at Rocky Ridge Farm.

Laura loved to preserve the mementos of her own past. Nearly every piece of paper she wrote on, each card or letter she ever received, all the family photographs ever taken—Laura kept them all. And, fortunately, most of Laura's belongings have been saved. Her Rocky Ridge farmhouse near Mansfield, Missouri, was not only the home of a famous author; it was also a repository of over a century of Ingalls-Wilder family life in the photo albums, documents, letters, newspaper clippings, and reminders of daily life both large and small that Laura saved. And throughout the places where Laura lived as a child, a string of museums has risen to preserve what can be seen of Ingalls-Wilder life in Wisconsin, Iowa, Minnesota, Kansas, New York State, Missouri, and South Dakota. To each of these places history has come trickling back—old photos, autograph albums, letters, legal documents, needlework, and clothing. From old trunks and attics, from descendants of Laura's family and friends—history comes back to remind us of Laura's life in the frontier era.

The contents of this book have been gathered from a variety of these museums, archives, and libraries, as well as private collections from coast to coast. Nothing can surpass Laura's eloquent way of leading us into the past through her words, but seeing these bits and pieces from her life itself can enhance our appreciation of the Little House stories and the woman who wrote them, and help us connect with our own pasts.

William Anderson, 1998

Grand parents

Father Colby died May 22 – 1857 aged 72 ys

Mother Colby died march 15 – 1862 aged 80 ys

Mother Ingalls died may the 6 – 1837 – aged 64 ys

Father Ingalls died Feb 15 – aged 70 years

Lansford W Ingalls was born Nov 12 – 1812

Laura Colby was born Nov 5 – 1810

Lansford W Ingalls was united in

marriage to Laura Colby   1832

Sons and Daughters born to them

Peter R Ingalls Born Oct 25 – 1833

Our babe was born Feb 18

Charles P Ingalls was bo

Lydia L Ingalls born

Poly M Ingalls born Oct

Lansford James born

Laura Ladocia born

Hiram L Ingalls born

George W Ingalls born

Ruby C Ingalls born

(above) Lansford and Laura Ingalls with some of their children. Seated are: Lydia Louisa, Laura, Lansford, and Ruby. Standing are: Lansford James, George, and Hiram. George and Hiram served in the Civil War.

BEFORE
LAURA'S TIME

aura Ingalls Wilder's family roots were those of the westward-moving pioneer. Laura's grandfather Lansford Ingalls was born in Canada, but as an adult he moved to New York State, where Laura's father, Charles Ingalls, was born in 1836. Charles was a young boy when he first heard the West being discussed, and stories of rich and fertile land on the frontier sparked his imagination. In the 1840s Charles and his family moved west into Wisconsin. There they settled near Concord and worked together on their new land.

(above) Lansford and Laura Colby Ingalls, Laura's grandparents. (far left) The family record of Lansford and Laura Colby Ingalls. Their third child, Charles Ingalls, was born in 1836.

(above) Charlotte Holbrook, Caroline Quiner's half-sister. She is Aunt Lottie in Little House in the Big Woods. (below) The Quiner-Holbrook family, circa late 1850s. From left: Frederick Holbrook, Thomas Quiner, Charlotte Holbrook, and Caroline's mother, Charlotte Quiner Holbrook.

(left) The autograph album of Charlotte Tucker, Caroline's mother, dates to the late 1820s and includes verses by her future husband, Henry Newton Quiner.

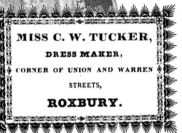

MISS C. W. TUCKER,
DRESS MAKER,
CORNER OF UNION AND WARREN
STREETS,
ROXBURY.

In Concord the Ingalls family befriended another big family clan that also had roots back east. Henry Newton and Charlotte Tucker Quiner had moved from Boston and New Haven all the way to the pioneer territory of Wisconsin in the 1830s. Like many pioneers, they had made the journey in stages. They had first settled in Ohio and then in Indiana, where their first children, Joseph, Martha, and Henry, were born. When they arrived in the frontier town of

(opposite, near right) Prior to her marriage in 1830 Charlotte was a dressmaker in the Roxbury section of Boston. This is an advertising card she used. The W stands for Wallis. (right) One of Caroline Quiner's student compositions, "The Ocean." She may have thought of her own father's death in a shipwreck as she penned these lines. (below) Caroline's teacher, Mary J. Moore, praised Caroline's diligent behavior in this school commendation.

The Ocean

What a world of beauty there is in the Ocean! Look upon it in a calm, and it fills us with awe and admiration. How it sparkles as the sun shines upon it in all its splendor, and how lovely and majestic the ships look sailing upon its smooth and placid surface. Imagine a ship coming into port, on a calm and pleasant day. A great number of people have congregated to witness the scene, and welcome their friends, who have been spared, to return in safty, to them after an absence of perhaps months. Then imagine a ship on the water in a storm. What a contrast! All is hurry and confusion on board; for every hand must be at work, to save the ship if possible. And how often the ship, and its whole crew, find a grave in the bed of the ocean, and become the food of animals of the deep. Who can picture the sufferings, of the survivors, on board a wreck? perhaps no more than three or four remains of some hundred persons and they must about at the mercy of the winds and waves, days, with hardly food enough to sustain some passing ship may pick them up is almost extinct; or perhaps after all ings and endeavors to get ashore; or attention of some passing ship they

Caroline

This certifies that Caroline L. Quiner for good behavior and attention to her studies merits my approbation and esteem
Mary J Moore

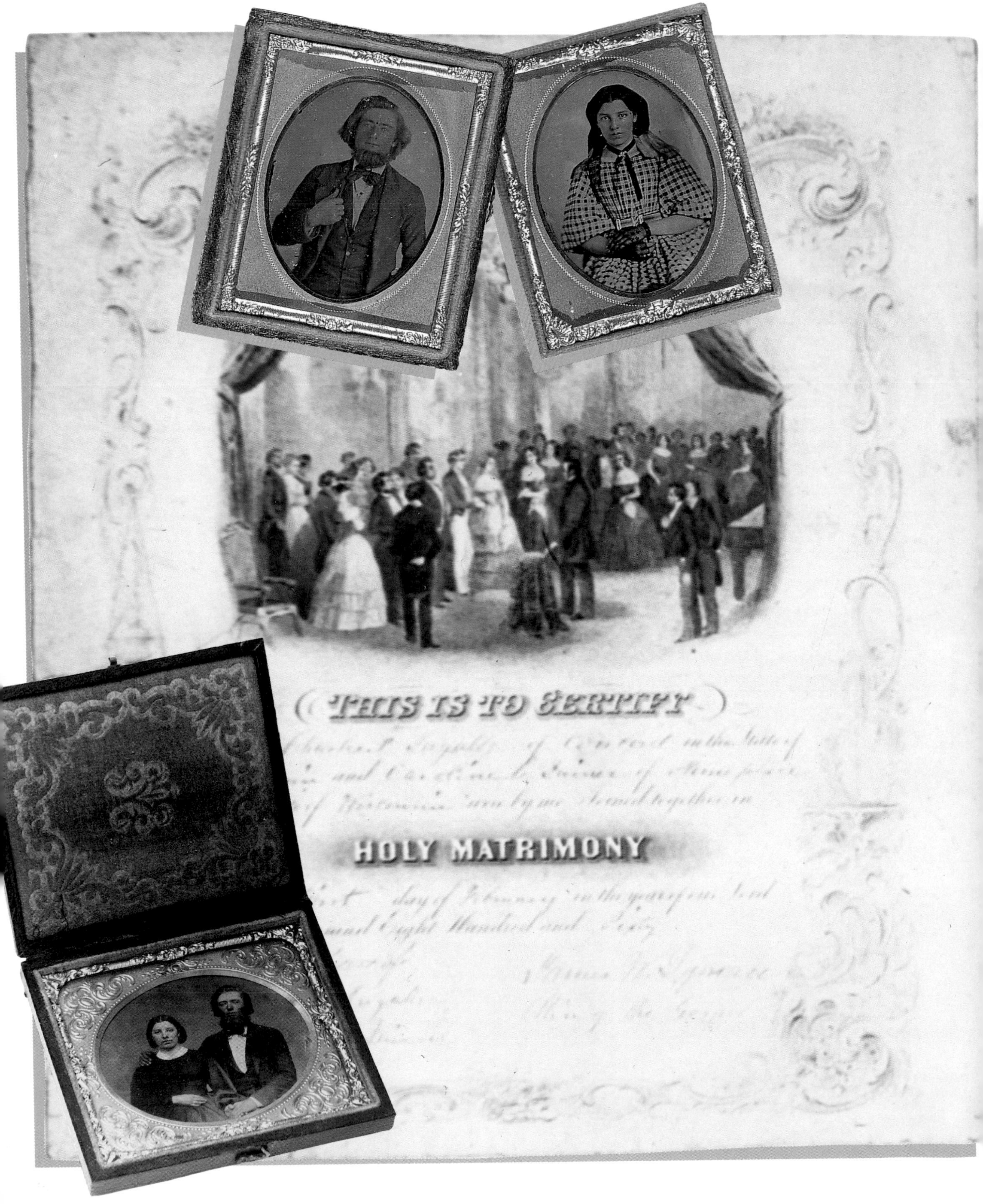

THIS IS TO CERTIFY

HOLY MATRIMONY

Brookfield, Wisconsin, in 1839, another daughter was born. She was named Caroline, and it is said she was the first non-Indian baby born in the vicinity. Then came Eliza and Thomas. Charlotte watched over the children while Henry went out on trading trips. He did a good business until, in 1844, a much longer trip took him by schooner to the Straits of Mackinac, in Michigan. A storm swamped the ship, and Henry, along with the rest of the crew, drowned. After a year or two Charlotte moved her family to Concord. There, in 1849, Charlotte married Frederick Holbrook and had one more child, whom she named Charlotte. And it was in Concord that the Quiner family met the Ingalls family.

During the 1850s the Quiner children and the Ingalls children attended the same school; they went to the same parties and dances and spelling bees. They skated on the frozen river in winter and waded and fished in summer. And romance developed between three pairs of the boys and girls. Polly Ingalls married Henry Quiner in 1859, Charles Ingalls married Caroline Quiner in 1860, and Peter Ingalls married Eliza Quiner in 1861. Martha, the only Quiner girl not to marry an Ingalls, married another neighbor, Charles Carpenter, in 1862.

(opposite, top) Two rare ambrotypes of the young Charles Ingalls and Caroline Quiner from their courting days, circa 1858–1859. Each of the small photos was encased in a black leather case. During the Civil War soldiers of both sides carried such small reminders of their loved ones at home. (opposite) Wedding certificate and wedding photograph of Caroline Quiner and Charles Ingalls, February 1, 1860.
(right) Peter and Eliza Quiner Ingalls, most likely in their wedding picture. They were close friends of Charles and Caroline, and the two couples' children, who were double cousins, looked so similar that they were sometimes mistaken for siblings.

Like a gigantic meadow spreads
the prairie wide and green
And here and there the violets
add a purple sheen.
The air is fresh and balmy and
little breezes sing,
In the Spring.

In the hush of early morn,
when the dew is on the grass
And bright hued clouds go sailing by,
as night-time shadows pass,
The world is full of music,
for the meadow larks sing,
In the Spring.

Laura Ingalls Wilder

MOVING WEST

n 1862, during the early days of the Civil War, the Ingalls family talked of moving farther west into the deep forests of Wisconsin. Charles and Caroline were eager to go; so were Henry and Polly. So the four of them stocked their covered wagons and traveled into the frontier. The wagon caravan traveled to the Mississippi River and stopped not far from the town of Pepin, Wisconsin.

In 1863 Charles and Caroline bought their own land about seven miles from Pepin. Their closest neighbors were Henry and Polly. Now there were new cabins to build, forests to clear, and land to plow. Charles and Henry traded work, hunted together, and farmed together. Caroline and Polly shared the difficult jobs of pioneer housekeeping.

(opposite) The Kansas prairie. (above) A modern-day replica of Laura's little house on the prairie.

(top) Lake Pepin, a widened section of the Mississippi River, looking across at the bluffs of Minnesota. (center) Eva and Clarence Huleatt were the children of Thomas and Maria Clarke Huleatt, close friends of Charles and Caroline. Their home was called Oakland and was a short walk from the Ingalls cabin. Eva and Clarence were among Laura and Mary's first childhood friends and appear in Little House in the Big Woods. (bottom) On long winter days and nights, when the family stayed safe and warm in the shelter of the cabin, Pa drew pictures for his daughters to enjoy.

(above) Pa's "Big Green Book," published in 1871, was entitled The Polar and Tropical Worlds. *With two hundred illustrations, it offered a rich and diverse view of the natural world beyond the Wisconsin woods. Later, in Dakota Territory, the Ingalls family identified an auk from the picture (right) of the bird in this book. Laura wrote about the incident in* The Long Winter.

Just before the Civil War ended, Caroline and Charles had their first baby. They called her Mary Amelia, and she was born on January 10, 1865. Two years later Laura Elizabeth was born on February 7, 1867. Their family was growing.

Though their farm in the woods gave them a comfortable harvest of crops, and the forest was full of game, Charles and Caroline were pioneers and used to moving on. When Laura was still just a baby, Charles and Caroline decided to seek their fortune farther west. With Mary and Laura they set out by covered wagon, traveling hundreds of miles until they stopped on the prairie near Independence, Kansas, in the heart of what was then called Indian Territory.

The Ingallses loved the prairie. However, because of the unrest in Indian Territory, many of the settlers started to leave the area, the Ingalls family among them. Fortunately, the family was able to return to their previous home. Charles had sold the farm near Pepin before leaving for Kansas, but the buyer could no longer pay for it. So the house and land were returned to Charles.

THE GIANT-AUK

Traveling once more by covered wagon, the Ingalls family, with their new baby, Carrie, reversed their previous journey and once again lived in the little house in the Big Woods near Pepin.

However, their traveling days were far from over. Laura's Pa longed for the wide-open prairie and fixed his mind this time on the flat lands of western Minnesota. In February 1874 Charles and Caroline set out again on another trip west. This time Peter and Eliza

(above) The Reverend Alden, who was the missionary pastor of the Walnut Grove church.
(right) Laura's china box. Laura describes the Christmas in the Walnut Grove church when she received this box in On the Banks of Plum Creek. *(below) The publication the Ingalls girls read eagerly.*

THE YOUTH'S COMPANION

VOLUME XLVII.

No. 41 TEMPLE PLACE.

NUMBER 17.

PERRY MASON & CO., PUBLISHERS.

BOSTON, THURSDAY, APRIL 23, 1874.

For the Companion.

TWO LETTERS;
OR, HOW AUNT KITTY'S HOUSE WAS BURNT AND BUILT.

By Julia A. Eastman.

The insurance policy ran out at twelve o'clock that night.

Two hours later, to wit, at two in the morning, that house took the opportunity to burn down, or burn up, whichever you please. It did both, I think, for it was old and dry, and it blazed up and reddened the sky. Dea. Frye, six miles off, saw the reflection, and told his wife that it was a clear case of Northern Lights, and the fact that it appeared directly in the south shook the good old man's belief not one jot.

And the house burnt down so furiously that ___ only time to seize her gray cat ___ ___ across the yard,

Aunt Kitty looks down at the small face and the child forehead knotted into hard knots of dis___ tress. It is Nix Maynard, the minister's si___ year-old daughter, and her question has remin___ ed Aunt Kitty for the first time of Rosa's untim___ ly end. Rosa was a large doll, with wonder___ garments, and both wardrobe and wearer w___ at the constant disposal of all young visitors ___ Miss Cranson's house.

"Yes, Nix, Rosa was burnt and every t___ else."

"The little dishes? And the baby-w___ And all the paper-dolls? And the rabbit-___ to make bunny 'blue-monge' in?"

Aunt Kitty says yes, and Nix goes aw___ of wonder and grief.

The truth is, the house that has gon___ smoke was the paradise of little folk___ Kitty loved children, and she filled h___ with them on all possible occasions.___ pose no building in New England ever___ so many birthday parties as the one___ burnt without insurance. It was pa___ cellar floor to chimney top with qua___ for juveniles.

The attic was rich in old-fashio___ high-waisted gowns, swallow-tailed ___ ___ two great shell combs; and ___ ___ worn a score of ___ (right) *Ma started her daughters early on housewifely arts. Laura remembered cooking on the trail when she was so small that she had to stand on a box to reach the camp table. Ma made all the family clothing and taught her girls to sew along with her. Mary was five when she started this quilt. Unfortunately, no one knows where the individual patches came from—perhaps a swatch from Grandma's dress, a piece of Pa's shirt, or a remnant of a dress Ma made before she married.*

(below) Pa was a merry fiddler, playing lively tunes by ear. It is a mystery how he acquired this violin—and learned to play it—on the edge of the frontier.

went with them. The two families traveled together until they reached eastern Minnesota. There Peter and his family stayed, but Charles and Caroline went right on, driving straight west all the way to the banks of Plum Creek, near the pioneer village of Walnut Grove.

The Ingalls family lived first in a dugout hollowed into the side of Plum Creek's bank, and then in a house made of store-bought lumber. The creek was a playground for the three sisters and their dog, Jack. Laura and Mary also started going to school, walking two miles to the school in Walnut Grove and two miles back each day.

The land was rich and fertile, and the Ingallses might have stayed indefinitely on the Minnesota prairie but for the

difficulties they had in starting a farm. Grasshopper invasions destroyed the wheat crops twice in the mid-1870s, leaving the family in debt and with little food to eat.

Those were hard times for the Ingalls family and their neighbors. Charles had to walk hundreds of miles to eastern Minnesota to find day-labor jobs in order to earn money for his family. The one bright spot in these dark years was the birth of a fourth child, Charles Frederick, on November 1, 1875.

The year 1876 brought no better crops, so Pa and Ma packed up their family and headed for a new life in Burr Oak, Iowa, where they would help operate a hotel. They stopped in Minnesota to visit Peter and Eliza and their family. On their journey east little Charles Frederick grew ill and eventually died, making the trip a sad one.

The hotel at Burr Oak was, at first, a comforting oasis to the sorrowful Ingalls family. Charles and Caroline worked in the hotel along with the owners, cooking and serving meals for the never-ending stream of people who passed through town in stagecoaches or covered wagons. Laura also helped out, running errands for the hotel's guests and looking after their children. Laura and Mary went to school, too, which this time was just one block away from where

(top left) The Burr Oak House, also known as the Masters Hotel. (above) Baby Grace Ingalls, who was born ten years after Laura.

FAMILY RECORD.

MARRIAGES

Married in Concord Jefferson
Co. Wisconsin, by Rev. J. W.
Lyman, Charles P. Ingalls
& Caroline L. Quiner, Feb. 1st
1860,

FAMILY RECORD.

BIRTHS.

Mary Amelia Ingalls born
Tuesday Jan. 10th 1865, Town, Pepin
Pepin Co. Wisconsin.
Laura Elizabeth Ingalls born
Thursday Feb. 8th 1867 Town of
Pepin Pepin Co. Wisconsin
Caroline Celestia Ingalls
born Wednesday Aug 3, 1870.
Montgomery Co Kansas.
Charles Frederic Ingalls Born
monday Nov. 1st 1875 Town North
Hero Redwood Co Minnesota.
Grace Pearl Ingalls born
Tuesday May 28th 1877 in the
Town of Burr Oak Winneshiek
Co. Iowa

they lived. And it was in Burr Oak that the fourth daughter
and last Ingalls child was born. Her name was Grace Pearl.

Eventually Charles and Caroline grew tired of the
noise and bustle of Burr Oak and decided to
return to Walnut Grove. There Pa built a new
little house for the family in a big pasture,
and worked as a carpenter and a butcher. It
was in this new home that tragedy struck. In
the winter of 1879, when Mary was fourteen, she
became very ill. Her disease, which was then called "brain fever," left her blind.

(above) The Ingalls family Bible, open to the pages of marriages and births, and an early piece of Laura's needlework.

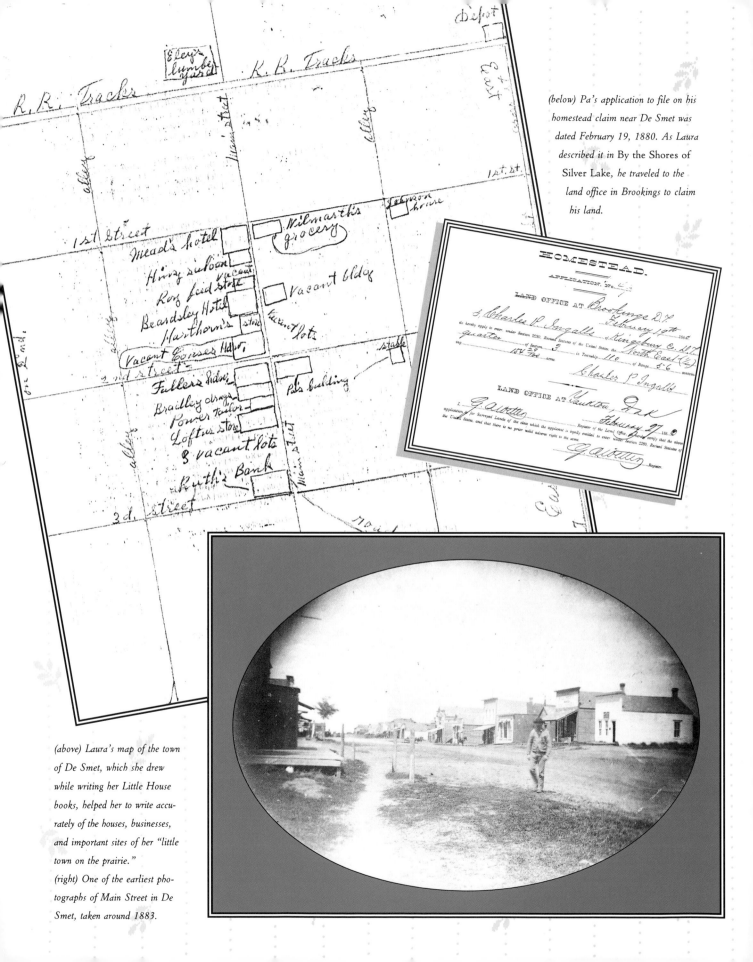

(below) Pa's application to file on his homestead claim near De Smet was dated February 19, 1880. As Laura described it in By the Shores of Silver Lake, *he traveled to the land office in Brookings to claim his land.*

(above) Laura's map of the town of De Smet, which she drew while writing her Little House books, helped her to write accurately of the houses, businesses, and important sites of her "little town on the prairie."

(right) One of the earliest photographs of Main Street in De Smet, taken around 1883.

THE LITTLE TOWN
ON THE PRAIRIE

The Ingalls family made their last move westward in the months leading up to 1880. The Chicago and Northwestern Railroad Company extended its train tracks from Minnesota into Dakota Territory, and a flood of new settlers followed. Pa, again longing to move on, got a job as timekeeper in the railroad construction camps, and he followed the work crews west until they reached the Silver Lake camp near the future town site of De Smet. Ma and the girls joined Pa there, and the Ingalls family became the first permanent settlers of De Smet.

(above) From left to right, Carrie, Mary, and Laura. This is the first photograph ever taken of the three girls.

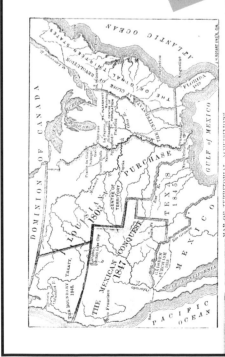

PA AND MA

"Account with Mrs White"

1 week .75
2 weeks 1.50 a week $ 3.00
4 yds calico 9 cts. a yard = .36
1 steele thimble .10
1 pair cloth shoes 1.00
½ yd. silk .25
1 plume .60
1 charm .10
Mrs Clayson for work .25
.36
.10
1.00

Laura E. Ingalls.

THE

MODEL HISTORY.

A BRIEF ACCOUNT OF THE

AMERICAN PEOPLE;

FOR SCHOOLS.

BY EDWARD TAYLOR, A.M.

"Nothing is really worth recording as final history except what promotes the permanent welfare of man."—PARTON.

CHICAGO:
GEORGE SHERWOOD & CO.

(above) A tintype of Charles and Caroline Ingalls, circa 1880. (top right) Laura was ambitious and eager to earn money to help Pa and Ma. Her first job in De Smet was sewing for Mrs. White, who owned a dry-goods business. This is Laura's handwritten account of her work for Mrs. White, described in Little Town on the Prairie. (center right) Easterners brought their fads and styles with them to the western prairies. Name cards were popular when Laura attended school in De Smet. As she recounted in Little Town on the Prairie, Laura exchanged this decorated name card with her friends. (right) Laura learned of the settling of America through this map in her history book, which she used in 1882–1883. (opposite, center) An engraving of the Iowa State College for the Blind as it looked while Mary attended it, 1881–1889.

During the winter of 1879–1880 the Ingalls family lived in the railroad company's Surveyors' House. For months they were alone, but in the spring homesteaders came flocking to the area to settle on their claims and start

IOWA INSTITUTION
FOR THE
EDUCATION OF THE BLIND.

(above) Eliza Jane Wilder, Laura's teacher in De Smet. In addition to teaching, she worked hard as a home-steader, establishing a home on the prairie.

businesses in De Smet. The Surveyors' House became a temporary hotel, simply because there was no other place to eat or sleep. Ma and the girls kept busy cooking for all the travelers pouring into the territory.

Out on the prairie a mile from the new town of De Smet, Pa Ingalls built a claim shanty for his family. He dug a well, built a stable, and planted crops. But the winter of 1880–1881 was so fierce

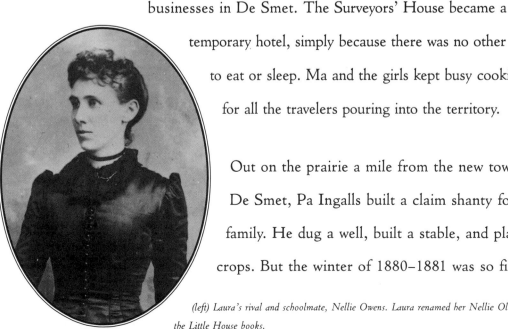

(left) Laura's rival and schoolmate, Nellie Owens. Laura renamed her Nellie Oleson in the Little House books.

that Pa had to move his family and livestock to town, where it would be easier to get supplies and food. Blizzards soon stopped the trains, and the stores ran out of food and fuel. So Pa and Laura twisted hay meant to feed the livestock into sticks to burn in the cookstove. Ma ground wheat to make coarse flour for daily bread. For months the Ingalls family huddled around the stove, grinding and twisting and waiting for spring. It was only because a young homesteader, Almanzo Wilder, and his friend Cap Garland, risked their lives to bring the town some extra wheat that no one starved to death.

(above, left) Church and Sunday school were important to the Ingalls family; Pa and Ma were among the founders of De Smet's First Congregational church. The Sunday school card was given to Laura as a reminder to abstain from alcohol, tobacco, and improper language. (above, right) Laura's first composition. She described the anxious moments she felt while writing this essay in These Happy Golden Years. Her teacher, Professor Owen, recognized her writing abilities and encouraged and helped her with her work. (left) Laura was always an outstanding scholar, and she received more than one "Reward of Merit" for her schoolwork.

The next year was a busy one.
Pa and Ma helped found the Congregational
church in De Smet, and Pa served on the school board. Laura and Carrie
started school again in the fall of 1881. Miss Eliza Jane Wilder, Almanzo
Wilder's sister, was their teacher. Laura did not care much for Miss
Wilder, but she liked school and was an excellent and popular student.

(above, left) Carrie, standing at left of the lamp, and a group of her friends in the 1890s. (above, right) One of Laura's paintings, done when she was a teenager. Laura painted a house in the woods to depict for Grace what trees were. Growing up on the prairie, Grace had no idea of forested regions. (left) Laura's first teaching certificate was issued to her two months before she reached the legal teaching age of sixteen.

No. 66   Department of Education.   COUNTY OF Kingsbury

TEACHER'S CERTIFICATE.

This is to Certify, that Miss Laura Ingalls

Has been examined by me, and found competent to give Instruction in

READING, ORTHOGRAPHY, WRITING, ARITHMETIC, ENGLISH GRAMMAR, GEOGRAPHY,

and having exhibited satisfactory testimonials of good moral character is authorized by this

Third Grade Certificate, to teach those branches in any Common School in the County, for the term of Twelve months.

Dated this 10th day of
December 188 3   Geo. A. Williams

Supt. of Schools, Kingsbury County, D. T.

RESULT OF EXAMINATION:
Reading. 62   Writing. 75   Orthography. 70   History. 89   English Grammar. 81   Arithmetic 80   Geography 70

Laura was determined to earn as much as she could to help Mary go to a school for the blind, so at fifteen she took her teacher's examination and accepted a contract to teach at a tiny school twelve miles from home. She was often homesick, but to her surprise Almanzo Wilder came driving out from De Smet every Friday to take her home to Pa and Ma for the weekend. Laura loved whizzing across the snowy prairie in Almanzo's swift cutter, drawn by two Morgan horses.

(above) Almanzo as a young De Smet homesteader. (below, left) Laura was seventeen when she posed for De Smet's pioneer photographer, Cooledge, in 1884. (below, right) During their courting days, Almanzo presented Laura with a gift book, Mother, Home & Heaven. *Laura inscribed the first page.*

(top) Almanzo's family, the Wilders. Before they left their farm in Malone, New York, to go west to Spring Valley, Minnesota, the Wilders posed for a photographer around 1871. Seated are: Royal, father James, Perley, mother Angeline, and Alice. Standing are Almanzo, Laura, and Eliza Jane. (above) Perley, Royal, and Almanzo in Spring Valley, Minnesota, around 1890. (right) Almanzo and his sister Alice were playmates and remained great friends all their lives.

Alice Wilder

(right) Mr. and Mrs. Almanzo J. Wilder, photographed the winter after they married. (bottom right) The marriage of Laura and Almanzo was noted in The De Smet News and Leader. *(bottom left) Almanzo was a good amateur carpenter and woodworker. For their first wedding anniversary he made Laura a little sewing box. The individual drawers were actually cigar boxes he had saved. (below)* The De Smet News and Leader *reported Rose's birth. (opposite) Rose Wilder, around four years old.*

—The good angels called at the home of Mr. and Mrs. A. J. Wilder, last Monday night, and left a bright little nine-pound girl to cheer their solitude. Dr. Cushman reports mother and daughter doing nicely. Grandpa Ingalls is entitled to wear gray hairs and numerous wrinkles now. "Manly" says they have named the little one Rose, and if she don't cause him many a "rose" during the cold, stilly watches of the night 'ere the balmy zephyrs of spring arrive, he may thank his lucky stars.

Parties calling for please say "advertised."

J. H. CARROLL, p. m.

MARRIED.

WILDER—INGALLS.—At the residence of the officiating clergyman, Rev. E. Brown, August 25, 1885, Mr. Almanzo J. Wilder and Miss Laura Ingalls, both of De Smet.

Thus two more of our respected young people have united in the journey of life. May their voyage be pleasant their joys be many and their sorrows few.

Harvest Picnic.

Laura earned forty dollars teaching her first school. She returned to De Smet and to her own classes at school. When spring arrived, Almanzo still came calling and took Laura riding in a buggy hitched to the beautiful brown Morgans.

While Laura and Carrie attended school in De Smet, Mary was far away studying. Pa and Ma enrolled her in the Iowa State College for the Blind at Vinton in 1881. There Mary learned to read and write Braille, made handicrafts, studied music, and pursued a college preparatory course. The family missed her greatly but was happy that Mary could continue her education.

Laura taught at two more schools, while Pa and Ma made the Ingalls claim look more like a farm. And as the Ingalls farm was growing, so too was the little town of De Smet. With Almanzo Wilder, Laura attended singing school,

socials, parties, and lectures. Laura and Almanzo were married on August 25, 1885, by the Reverend Edward Brown. After a wedding dinner with Laura's family, Laura and Almanzo drove to their own new home, a pretty gray house that Almanzo had built on his tree claim. Laura, well taught by Ma, soon mastered the tasks of running her own household. And on December 5, 1886, Laura and Almanzo became parents. Their daughter was named Rose, for the wild roses that covered the prairie in early summer.

Schofield, · Spring Valley, Minn.

...Lindsay,
Freddie Wright,
braska, | Emery Clark,
poultry | Sam Fuller,
g such | Ethel McNaughton.
f they
s dur- PRIMARY.
ed that Ray Jewell,
those Allie Gleason,
instead Willie Lattin,
Charlie Greenman,
meet- May Hanson,
Sunday Bertha Clark,
follows: Josie Bush,
Ruthie Davies,
ing by Madge Cornwell,
Christ, Martha Wilmarth,
Bertie Wright,
Paul. Ethel Keating.

C. A. JAMES A. FARRELL,
Principal.

For Sale or Trade.
An incubator nearly new.
sell or trade it. Apply to
202-3 E. GOMER DAVIES.
Millet Seed.

Robert Fuller,
Harold Tinkham,
Florence Hanson,
Maude May.

Pupils perfect in attendance, punctuality and
deportment:
Charlie Gipson,
Rose Wilder,
George Willard,
Claude Fuller,
Mabel Eckersley,
May Wright,
Tosie Loftus,
Dale Van Hook,
Alice Greenman,
Harry Wilmarth,
Carrie Drake.

AT

SYMP

COOLEDGE
DE SMET. S. DAK.

D. H. LOFTUS. W. E. BROADBENT.
Loftus & Broadbent
DE SMET, DAK.
NEW INVOICES!
For Fall & Winter Wear
DRESS STUFFS
BOOTS AND SHOES
UNDERWEAR
YANKEE NOTIONS.
DRESS TRIMMINGS.

1890 1900

FINDING A HOME

For Laura and Almanzo Wilder, farming on the Dakota prairie was a harsh experience. Drought, hail, fire, illness, and debt plagued them during the first four years of their married life. A baby son was born in 1889 but soon died; then a fire destroyed the Wilder tree-claim house. Because Almanzo was left nearly lame by an illness—probably polio—it was impossible for him to continue the strenuous work of a wheat farmer, and he and Laura decided to take respite from the hard winters and hot summers of South Dakota.

(opposite, clockwise from top left) The De Smet News and Leader *noted Rose's perfect attendance in school in 1894. A Congregational church Sunday school program in June 1894 included Rose Wilder, standing fourth from the left, just behind the flag. An advertisement from the De Smet paper; Mr. Loftus is mentioned several times in* The Long Winter. *This photograph of the Ingalls family was probably taken just before Laura's departure from the family circle in 1894. She stands, in her black wedding dress, with hand on Pa's shoulder. Ma is at the left, Mary at right. Standing on either side of Laura are Carrie, at left, and Grace, at right. (above) Laura and Almanzo in the piney woods of Florida, 1891 or 1892.*

In 1890 Laura, Almanzo, and Rose went to Spring Valley, Minnesota, to spend a year with Almanzo's parents. Almanzo slowly recovered from his illness, but he was told warm weather would speed his recovery, so in 1891 the Wilders journeyed to Florida. They were homesick for the west, though, and soon returned to De Smet. There they lived in town, and worked and saved money for a new start somewhere else.

At around this time the Ozark Mountains of Missouri were opening up to development, and the Wilders heard stories of the mild climate and fertile land. So in 1894, with a $100 bill they had saved for a claim, Laura, Almanzo, and Rose climbed into a loaded black-painted covered wagon and left the prairie for good.

Laura and Almanzo were full of hope that they would at last be able to settle down on a farm. And when the family arrived in the little village of Mansfield, they knew they had found their new home. They bought a farm just a mile east of the town square. It had a running creek, apple trees, and a rough little log house. Laura named it Rocky Ridge Farm.

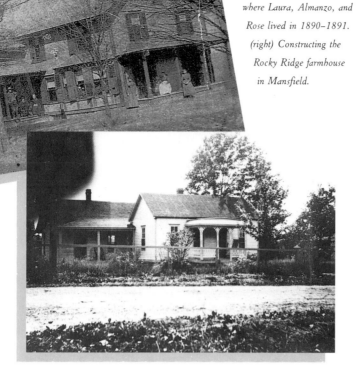

(left) The Wilder family home in Spring Valley, Minnesota, where Laura, Almanzo, and Rose lived in 1890–1891. (right) Constructing the Rocky Ridge farmhouse in Mansfield.

(left) Laura and Almanzo's town house in Mansfield. (below) Rose and her donkey, Spookendyke, with the apple orchard of Rocky Ridge in the background.

On their forty-acre farm Laura and Almanzo planted crops and a garden, milked cows, and sold eggs from their flock of chickens. During the early years the farm showed so little profit that the Wilders moved to Mansfield to work. Almanzo ran a delivery service, and Laura cooked for railroad men. She also took in boarders. Their little house in town was on the road to Rocky Ridge Farm, which they frequently visited, and close to the school where Rose soon became an outstanding scholar.

(opposite, counterclockwise from top) Ma in 1897, Pa in 1894, Mary, Laura, Carrie, and Grace.

De Smet S D

Oct 16 1904

Mrs E L Green Libby Iowa

Dear Friend I had thought to write to you before this time but we h... been so busy that I did ... time. We were glad to ... letter. It was nice of ...er to write to me. I feel ... ... is my friend ... ... to her before she writes ... ... ove and best wishes ... ... without you and ... ... soon even home ... ... and your ... ... may ever true ... ... change in the ... ... of yours

Mary Ingalls

Mary A. Ingalls.

Woman's Missionary Society

Congregational Church, De Smet, S. D.

Outline of Work for 1905

February — **Alaska**
Leader, Mrs. Henney   Hostess, Mrs. Danley

March — **China's Dynasties**
Leader, Mrs. Cooledge   Hostess, Mrs. Garland

April — **Chinese Provinces and Map Drill**
Leader, Mrs. Stiles   Hostess, Mrs. Richardson

May — **The Religions of China**
Leader, Mrs. Darley   Hostess, Mrs. Henney

June — **The People of China**
Leader, Mrs. Morgan   Hostess, Mrs. Hubbard

July — **Christian Mission's in China, 1 and 2 Period**
Leader, Mrs. Benedict   Hostess, Mrs. Stiles

August — **Christian Missions, 3 Period**
Leader, Mrs. Johnson   Hostess, Mrs. Johnson

September — **Christian Missions, 4th Period**
Leader, Mrs. Wright   Hostess, Mrs. Benedict

October — **China the Open Door of Opportunity**
Leader, Mrs. Hubbard   Hostess, Mrs. Wright

November — **Work Among the Philippinos**
Leader, Miss Ingalls   Hostess, Mrs. Ingalls

December — **Mormonism**
Leader, Mrs. Richardson   Hostess, Mrs. Morgan

Meetings the first Friday of each month at 3 p. m.

MRS. EVA COOLEDGE, President.

All are Cordially Welcome.

OLD AND NEW TIES

Before Laura left De Smet to live in Mansfield, Pa and Ma and her sisters had settled in town for good. The homestead was sold, and Pa built the family's final home on Third Street. It was a cozy frame house, which Pa first constructed in 1887 and later added to and improved. After Mary graduated from the Iowa State College for the Blind in 1889, she returned to De Smet to live with Ma and Pa. Carrie and Grace finished school, and both helped to support the family. Grace taught, and Carrie learned the printing trade at *The De Smet News and Leader.*

In 1901 Grace married Nate Dow, a farmer from the nearby town of Manchester. After their wedding at the Ingalls home, the Dows settled on their farm, which was seven miles from De Smet.

(opposite) Mary wrote to seeing friends in pencil on a grooved slate, which enabled her to keep lines straight. This 1904 letter was to Minnie Green, a close friend and neighbor from De Smet. (opposite, center left) Mary's calling card. (opposite, bottom left) The Ingalls family was always active in De Smet's Congregational church. Ma and Mary hosted a missionary program in November 1905. (above) Mansfield's Main Street in the early 1900s.

A Pioneer Gone.

The people of De Smet were pained Sunday afternoon to learn of the death of Mr. C. P. Ingalls, who died at 3 p. m. of that day after a lingering illness of several weeks. Heart trouble was the cause of his death.

Funeral services were held at the Congregational church Tuesday forenoon, largely attended by the many friends of the deceased and of the family. After the church services were concluded the Masonic fraternity, who were in attendance in a body, took charge of the funeral and the remains were placed in their last resting place with the solemn funeral rites of that organization.

Charles P. Ingalls was born in the state of New York sixty years ago. His life was that of the pioneer from his boyhood. At the age of twelve years he moved with his parents to Illinois, thence, a few years later, to Wisconsin, and thence to Minnesota. It was while living in Wisconsin that he married the estimable lady who is now his widow. In 1879 he brought his family to what is now De Smet. He was the first to build a dwelling ing in this locality, the house that now stands on the rear end of the Bank of De Smet lot is the building. In his home were held the first religious services. He was prominent in the work of organizing the Congregational church in this city, of which he was a faithful and consistent member at the time of his death. He was also a member in good standing of the Masonic order and of O. E. S.

As a citizen he was held in high esteem, being honest and upright in his dealings and associations with his fellows. As a friend and neighbor he was always kind and courteous and as a husband and father he was faithful and loving. And what better can be said of any man? Some few accomplish great things in life's short span; they control the destinies of nations, or hold in their hand, as it were, the wealth of the world; but the great many tread the common walks of life and to them falls the work of making the world better. He who does this work well is the truly great man. Such was he who has lately been called to the Great Beyond. Charles P. Ingalls did his life's work well and the world is better for his having lived in it.

There remain to mourn his death a wife and four daughters, Mrs. Laura Wilder, Mrs. Grace Dow, and Misses Carrie and Mary Ingalls. To the bereaved is extended the heartfelt sympathy of all in this community.

(above) Pa's obituary appeared in
The De Smet News and Leader
after his death on June 8, 1902.

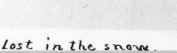

MANCHESTER.

The Presbyterian Ladies Aid met with Mrs. Chas. Spear Wednesday.

Mrs. Will Howard is visiting her sister, Mrs. George Montany, who lives near Blunt, N. D. She will be gone about a month.

Mr. Bjornson and W. Keller left Thursday for North Dakota to look over the land with the idea of investing.

Mrs. N. W. Dow has been enjoying a visit from her sister, Mrs. A. J. Wilder, of Mansfield, Missouri.

Lost in the snow. April 30, 1903

Pa became seriously ill in 1902, and from far-off Missouri Laura traveled by train to see him one last time. Before he died, Pa told Laura that she was to have his fiddle. She had loved his music and songs perhaps more than anyone else, and they were her legacy from a pioneer father. She was with Pa when he died, and she stayed on for his funeral and a visit with Ma and her sisters.

After Pa's death Ma, Mary, and Carrie remained in the house on Third Street. Carrie continued to work as a printer and newspaperwoman, and she also claimed a prairie homestead near Philip, in western South Dakota. For six months during each year from 1905 to 1908, Carrie lived at Ma's house. The other six months she stayed on her claim to "hold it down." While she ran *The Keystone Recorder*

(opposite, top center) Ma in the parlor at home, circa 1905. Carrie took this photograph with a box camera and developed the picture herself. Pa's portrait hangs on the wall. (opposite, top right) Ma often sent postcard greetings to Laura on birthdays and holidays. (opposite, bottom center) Grace sent this photograph of herself and her husband to Laura. (opposite, bottom right) This clipping from the local newspaper in Manchester records Laura's 1902 visit to Grace. (above) Carrie's claim shanty, north of Philip, South Dakota. Ma wrote on this photo, "Carrie's claim. She has an acre fenced, sod coal house by shanty 10 x 12 feet boarded up a little in the ground." (left) Carrie ran presses, set type, wrote news, and edited the paper. Here she is in one of the many frontier newspaper offices that she operated through western South Dakota.

and the *Hill City Star* in the Black Hills, she was courted by a mine owner and prospector named David Swanzey. He and Carrie were married in Rapid City in 1912. They settled in Keystone, and there Carrie became a second mother to Mr. Swanzey's two young children, Mary and Harold.

Mr. and Mrs. Almanzo J. Wilder
announce the marriage of their daughter
Rose
to
Mr. Claire Gillette Lane
Wednesday, March the twenty fourth
one thousand nine hundred and nine
San Francisco

(above, left and right) Rose posed for graduation photos during her last year of school in Crowley, Louisiana, in 1904. (left) Although Laura and Almanzo did not attend Rose's wedding, they sent out this announcement to friends and family.

(opposite) Laura and Rose both had their photographs taken in Kansas City in October 1906. (opposite, bottom) Almanzo and his brother Perley on Rocky Ridge Farm. They are riding mules, which were better suited to the flinty terrain than horses.

The Ingalls and Wilder families heard from Laura and Almanzo what an outstanding student Rose was. Rose needed academic challenges that the local Mansfield school could not offer. During 1903–1904 Rose lived with Almanzo's sister Eliza Jane Thayer in Crowley, Louisiana, and attended the rigorous high school there. At graduation exercises Rose addressed the group with an original poem she had composed in Latin.

Rose came home to Mansfield and learned telegraphy at the little railroad station. Then, at seventeen, she moved to Kansas City and became a "bachelor girl,"

working as a telegraph operator. Her skill enabled her to travel, and she worked all over the country until she moved to San Francisco in 1908. A year later she married Gillette Lane in "the city by the bay."

The Improved Downs Patent Self-Adjusting Corset.

(above) The Rocky Ridge farmhouse, soon after it was completed
in 1913. The rustic grape arbor is near the rear door.

(above right) An advertising card.

ROCKY RIDGE FARM

Hard work, careful economy, and an inheritance from Almanzo's parents enabled Laura and Almanzo to move back to Rocky Ridge Farm and finish building the farmhouse. From native timber they raised a sturdy frame to add to the existing little house. Laura planned the addition; Almanzo and local workmen did the construction. It rose up from the rocky soil as if it belonged there, a comfortable, rustic, unique house, with old oak trees shading it and a wooded Ozark mountain behind it.

Over time Laura and Almanzo expanded Rocky Ridge Farm to almost 200 acres. It became known as a model farm in the region, and the Wilders became known

(left, bottom) Laura enjoyed entertaining in her newly completed farmhouse. This 1913 photo included, from left, Laura, Daisy Carnall, Mrs. John Freeman and her grandchildren, Meroe Andrews, and Sophia Freeman Quigley. (above) Laura around 1917, at the age of fifty.

(below, top) The stone fireplace that Laura designed for the parlor was made from stones found on the farm. (below, center) The parlor was finished with oak paneling and heavy beams, in the style of architect Frank Lloyd Wright.

as progressive farmers. Laura was often asked to present papers and demonstrations on her poultry-raising methods at farmers' meetings and organizations, and this gave her a modest fame in the area. Around 1910 she began submitting articles on poultry to the *St. Louis Star Farmer*, and in 1911 she published her first article in the *Missouri Ruralist*.

(above, left) Laura's first national exposure as a writer was an article on the lives of farm wives in the June 1919 issue of McCall's Magazine. (above, center) Mansfield's Justamere Club asked Laura to write the words for the club song, "We're All Good Friends." (above, right) Almanzo appeared on the cover of the Missouri Ruralist, *which published an article on the apple orchard at Rocky Ridge, in 1912.*

In her country journalism Laura shared tips for rural living and promoted the virtues and benefits of farm life. Her cheery outlook came through in the printed word, and she was considered an expert on farm families. Laura helped form literary societies for farm women throughout southwest Missouri, and she was active in both the Justamere club of Mansfield and The Athenians of Hartville.

(left) Ma's letters to Laura included household tips and news of life in De Smet. (opposite, third from top) Almanzo built a sideboard for dishes in the dining room, with a convenient pass-through to the kitchen. (opposite, top right) Laura began collecting these colorful advertisements in the 1880s. (opposite, bottom) Rocky Ridge under construction.

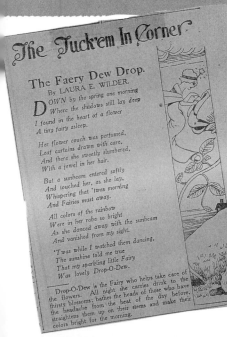

BUY MAY'S NORTHERN GROWN SEEDS.

L. L. MAY & CO., SEEDSMEN, ST. PAUL, MINN.

(left) Another of Laura's advertising cards. (below, left) Laura wrote several poems that were published in the San Francisco Bulletin, *in the "Tuck'em In Corner" section. (below, right) Rose's bookplate. (bottom right) Rose in 1915. (opposite, top left) A souvenir that Laura brought home from a restaurant in San Francisco. (opposite, top right) Laura with Rose's husband, Gillette Lane. (opposite, bottom) Laura sent home many postcards to Almanzo telling him all about her trip. She signed the cards "Bessie," which is what Almanzo called her.*

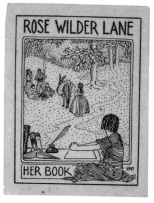

ROSE WILDER LANE

HER BOOK

The Tuck'em In Corner

Naughty Four O' Clocks

By LAURA INGALLS WILDER.

There were some naughty flowers once,
Who were careless in their play;
They got their petals torn and soiled
As they swung in the dust all day.

Then went to bed at four o'clock,
With faces covered tight,
To keep the fairy, Drop O' Dew
From washing them at night.

Poor Drop O' Dew! What could she do?
She said to the Fairy Queen,
"I cannot get those Four o'Clocks
To keep their faces clean."

The mighty Storm King heard the tale;
"My winds and rain," roared he,
"Shall wash those naughty flowers well,
As flowers all should be."

So raindrops came and caught them all
Before they went to bed,
And washed those little Four o'Clocks
At three o'clock instead.

The Tuck'em In Corner

The Faery Dew Drop.
By LAURA E. WILDER.

DOWN by the spring one morning
Where the shadows still lay deep
I found in the heart of a flower
A tiny fairy asleep.

Her flower couch was perfumed,
Leaf curtains drawn with care,
And there she sweetly slumbered,
With a jewel in her hair.

But a sunbeam entered softly
And touched her, as she lay,
Whispering that 'twas morning
And Fairies must away.

All colors of the rainbow
Were in her robe so bright
As she danced away with the sunbeam
And vanished from my sight.

'Twas while I watched them dancing,
The sunshine told me true
That my sparkling little Fairy
Was lovely Drop-O-Dew.

Drop-O-Dew is the Fairy who helps take care of the flowers. All night she carries drink to the thirsty blossoms; bathes the heads of those who have the headache from the heat of the day before, straightens them up on their stems and make their colors bright for the morning.

In the evenings Laura and Almanzo relaxed. Friends dropped in for supper, and sometimes Laura and Almanzo went to dances. Laura said she always had a little music in her feet. At home the Wilders listened to music on their Victrola, a gift from Rose, and shared books and magazines with each other.

Laura and Almanzo also eagerly followed their daughter's career. Rose became one of the first female real estate agents in California. Then, in 1915, she drifted into newspaper writing for the *San Francisco Bulletin.*

Rose wrote serial fiction stories for the *Bulletin,* interviewed San Franciscans, and reported on farmers and their lives in the countryside of California. She also helped Laura write

poems for young readers, which were published in the children's section of the newspaper.

In 1915 the great San Francisco Panama-Pacific Exposition opened, and Rose, who had not seen her parents in several years, invited them to visit. Almanzo did not feel he could leave the farm, so Laura set out alone. She traveled by train and wrote Almanzo frequent postcards and letters along the way. In San Francisco, sightseeing, touring the fair, dining in quaint cafés, and exploring the city on foot and by streetcar filled Laura and Rose's days.

Laura also closely observed the way in which Rose practiced the writer's craft, as she was ambitious to expand her own modest career as a journalist. Toward the end of her two-month visit Laura received assignments from the *Missouri Ruralist* to write reports on innovative agricultural practices being promoted at the fair.

Tower of Jewels, Panama-Pacific International Exposition, San Francisco, 1915.—The height of this great tower can hardly be realized from the picture. It is 433 feet high. Above the great columns on either side of the archway are four figures by John Flanagan—the Soldier, the Priest, the Philosopher and the Adventurer, moving types of the Renaissance.

the exposition is simply wonderful so beautiful in every way. Monday I shall see "the Dogs of

Love Rose

POST CARD

A. J. Wilder
Mansfield
Missouri

(left) The rock house, built in 1928 as a retirement cottage for Laura and Almanzo.
(below) The Wilders' first car: a 1923 blue Buick, which they named Isabelle. The car is shown in Colorado on a trip taken by Laura, Rose, and Rose's author friend Helen Boylston.
(bottom) Almanzo was a dedicated horseman all his life. His favorite breed was the Morgan, which he declared was well suited to the Ozarks. In 1925 Almanzo posed with the Governor of New Orleans, a handsome dark bay.

1920 1930

THE MIDDLE YEARS

$\mathcal{L}$aura and Almanzo did their share in the effort to win World War I: They were active in the local Red Cross work and geared their farming to raise needed commodities. In the years that followed the end of the war, Laura wrote of patriotism, thrift, and compassion for the victims of the war. Laura wrote steadily for the *Missouri Ruralist* and had her own columns— first "The Farm Home," then "As a Farm Woman Thinks."

In her community of Mansfield Laura suggested that the Methodist church hold its first bazaar, and whenever a social

(above) Laura. (right) Nero, one of Laura and Almanzo's many dogs.

A Merry Christmas

My Ozark Kitchen

By LAURA INGALLS WILDER

TTLE DOOR LEADS TO THE DINING-ROOM SIDEBOARD

OUR REMADE KITCHEN IS MOSTLY CABINETS AND WINDO

WHILE YOU ARE KNEADING YOU CAN ENJOY THIS
VIEW OF HILLS AND WOODS AND PASTURE

whole front of ever
a door one whisk
sweeps out the cup
are no corners to clu
no maddening obstacle
it must be lifted wit
broom.

Beginning with such windows and such cupb
only problem that remained was to arrange
meet the needs of a farm kitchen.
The east wall looks toward the barn
glimpse of wooded hill beyond it, a
orchard and pastures to the nort
of this wall not occupied by the
glass back door is filled by a
double window and the barn
boards. These cupboards are un
the sixteen-inch-wide window sill

Places for Everything

THE swill buckets for the pigs, the
skimmed milk for the hens, the
lanterns and the kerosene can all have
their places in these cupboards. There
is a shelf for the shoe-blacking outfit.
The cupboard doors shut them all out of
sight.
On the top of these low cupboards is a hand
basin and a jar of soft water. A towel rack is
fastened to the window casing and a small mirror
hangs against the double window.
Here I wash my hands and tidy my hair after excur-
sions to the henhouse or hasty dashes to settle the af-
fairs of colts or dogs. Here, too, the men wash up when
they come in to meals on cold days. Here, too, on
mornings I wash the lamps on
I set them from the oil
I let

start with
n we re-
uilding
house.
been
better.
en's
perfect room in which to
it was not what I
at a farm kitchen
tchen; it is the
et—often in
tchen was
placed
smells
st of

ntens'
r oil lamps,
problems. And
re accustomed to using our brains;
them in our work. That is one
advantages of living on a farm.
nsatisfactory kitchen was a
or room and junkshop com-
been meeting the barn, and
rom coming farther into
d weather the skimmed milk and the
ze and have to be brought in to
I studied this room for some
finish it up for a kitchen.
y good jackknife car-
er before that
could lessen
we did.
took us

or above to be dusted. They are all closed with light
doors, made of wall board framed in wood.
Every floor cupboard has a floor of its ow
broad three-quarter-inch board fo
and sloped to it at the

With
All Good
Wishes
for
a Merry
Christmas.
To Laura
From Mother

Merry Christmas
tings
To SISTER

There's no one else
who means to me
Just what my sister means!
No one whose mind
can go with me
Back to the old home scenes,
Who knows just how
our mother looked
When we were little things;
And Sister dear,
a world of cheer
I hope this Christmas
brings
to you.

Best Christmas wishes to
you and Manley from us all.

was held, she baked huge pans of her gingerbread, which became famous throughout the county. Each month Almanzo drove her to Hartville to attend meetings of The Athenians, which was a literary and study-oriented club. Laura regularly entertained the group at Rocky Ridge Farm.

During the 1920s Laura served as Secretary-Treasurer of the Mansfield Farm Loan Association. The association offered low-interest loans to Ozark farmers for improving or adding to their acreage. Laura had an office in town, where she explained the loans to farmers, kept records, and handled the finances. When an examiner arrived from Washington to audit the books, he reported that Laura's work was "neatly and accurately kept."

Rose, meanwhile, was traveling all over the world as a journalist and author. She saw much of Europe and the Near East; she explored the deserts of Egypt, the mountains of Albania, the islands of Greece, and the great cities of London, Vienna, Paris, Rome, and Athens.

Laura E. Wilder

Executive Office
State House
Jefferson City, Missouri

FREDERICK D. GARDNER
GOVERNOR

October 18th, 1920.

Mrs. A. J. Wilder,
c/o The Missouri Ruralist,
Wright City,
Missouri.

My dear Mrs. Wilder:-

I want to take this occasion to express to you my appreciation of the kind things you have to say in regard to my administration in your article in the Missouri Ruralist of October 5th.

I assure you that I deeply appreciate your kind expressions contained in your little editorial very, very much.

With kindest personal regards, I beg to remain,

Faithfully yours,

Frederick D. Gardner
Governor.

CLUB SONG

ATHENIANS

We're bound together by the ties,
Of friendship's trust and learning's quest;
The fires of ancient Greece still burn
Tended by daughters of the west;
So when the voice of knowledge speaks
On willing ears its accents fall
And when the tones of friendship call
All for one and one for all,
Athenians! Athenians!

Life's joys are sweeter when our friends
Are true of heart, mind tuned to mind:
Knowledge grows greater shared with those
Who gladly make return in kind;
And so together hand in hand
We journey onward, in the light
Of friendship's smile, t'ward wisdom's height,
Knowledge is power and love is might.
Athenians! Athenians!

(Composed by Mrs. A. J. Wilder)

(opposite, clockwise from bottom left) A Christmas greeting from Ma to Laura. Laura's first article in the nationally read Country Gentleman dealt with her kitchen on Rocky Ridge Farm. In 1919 Grace and her husband moved to the Ingalls home in De Smet to live with Ma and Mary. Grace sent this card to the Wilders from the folks in De Smet.
(right, top to bottom) Laura's calling card, probably while she was administrator of the Mansfield Farm Loan Association. Laura's work with the Missouri Ruralist was recognized by the governor of the state. Laura was asked to compose these words for The Athenians.

A VIEW FROM UPPER MAIN STREET—MALONE, N. Y.

Packages and letters and postcards streamed back to Rocky Ridge Farm from Rose, as Laura and Almanzo followed news of their daughter's treks. For three years Rose explored the world, storing up experiences for her writing at home.

(counterclockwise, from top left) Rose's travels took her to strange and familiar places; on one trip she visited Malone, New York, near her father's boyhood home. Rose labeled this picture in Egypt "Me and the Sphynx." Rose on the main avenue of Tirana, Albania, with a minister of the government. Wherever she traveled, Rose sought out the local people.

In 1923 Rose returned to Rocky Ridge Farm for a two-year stay. In her upstairs room her typewriter clattered continually as she wrote books and magazine stories. With the checks she earned from writing, Rose helped Laura and Almanzo improve the farm. Rose's own dream was to return to Albania, and in 1926 to 1928, with her friend Helen Boylston, a nurse and writer, Rose lived in the capital city of Tirana.

HOTEL
LASSEN

OWNED & OPERATED BY
THE RIGBY-GRAY HOTEL CO.

WICHITA, KANSAS

OPENED JANUARY 1919

9/18, 1925

Dear Manly,

We got to Wichita last night. We had to detour all over the state of Kansas because they were working on the highway so we did not get here until the sun had set and the stars come out, but we were in time for late supper. It had been a hard day so we are staying over a day to rest. The hotel is nice and comfortable and Isabell has behaved well all the time so far.

I had forgotten what sunset and star light was like on the prairie and the girls had never seen anything like it, or rather Rose did

(from bottom right) The Franklin Academy in Malone was the high school the Wilder children attended. Rose sent this postcard to Almanzo during her visit. On a trip through Minnesota Rose stopped in Spring Valley, where the Wilders had lived. The Methodist church was the congregation the family had attended. This photograph of Rose was taken during a walking tour of France. On a trip to California with Rose and Helen Boylston in 1925, Laura wrote to Almanzo about the journey.

M.E. CHURCH
SPRING VALLEY, MINN.

FRANKLIN ACADEMY, MALONE, N.Y.

But Rocky Ridge Farm once again beckoned. Rose returned home and soon sold a magazine serial with an Ozarks setting to *Country Gentleman* for $10,000, which made her one of America's best-paid writers. With her writing earnings Rose had a beautiful modern rock house built for her parents on a hillside of the family farm. Rose gave the house key to Laura and Almanzo for Christmas. They moved in, and Rose arranged the old farmhouse as her own home and writing workplace. Rocky Ridge became less a farm and more a home of writers.

By the author of "LITTLE HOUSE IN THE BIG WOODS"

LITTLE HOUSE ON THE PRAIRIE

LAURA INGALLS WILDER

Drawings by HELEN SEWELL

HARPER & BROTHERS   ESTABLISHED 1817

(above) Little House on the Prairie, *Laura's third book, published in 1935.*

The original illustrator of the series was Helen Sewell; another illustrator, Mildred Boyle, later joined her as a collaborator when Sewell became ill.

THE
LITTLE HOUSE BOOKS

*L*aura was past sixty when she and Almanzo moved into the rock house; they were both ready to give up the strenuous life of farming. Laura retired from her farm loan work, and her contributions to the *Missouri Ruralist* dwindled. Other writing ideas filled Laura's head. On lined school tablets, in pencil, Laura wrote of her frontier life with Pa and Ma. She called her book "Pioneer Girl," and when she finished it, she shared her work with Rose.

Rose was constantly at work on articles, magazine stories, and books, but she

(top) Laura in 1936, at the age of 69. (right) A Sewell illustration from On the Banks of Plum Creek.

GEORGE T. BYE
INCORPORATED
535 FIFTH AVENUE
New York

Telephone: MUrray Hill 2-8775   Cable Address: Byenbye

December 9, 1931.

Dear Mrs. Wilder:

Harpers are delighted to accept
"Little House in the Woods", and we are pleased to for-
ward you the contracts herewith.

There are three copies of the con-
tract, one for you, one for the publisher, and one for us.

I think you will find it in order.

Kindest wishes.

Faithfully yours,

Mrs. Laura Ingalls Wilder,
Rocky Ridge Farm,
Mansfield, Missouri.

FIFTY FIFTY
50 ⚫ 50
Springfield Grocer Co.
Springfield, Mo.

(far left) George T. Bye of New York City was the literary agent for both Laura and Rose. He handled their business with publishers. Mr. Bye also represented Eleanor Roosevelt, who would become the nation's First Lady. (near left) Laura penciled most of her books on nickel school tablets with the "Fifty Fifty" label. (bottom) Helen Sewell's picture of Ma, Pa, and Black Susan from Little House in the Big Woods.

took time to type Laura's handwritten manuscript and showed it to publishers in New York. Editors found the story of Laura's frontier life fascinating, but no one could discover a way to successfully publish it. It was a book about a girl, but it sounded as if it was for adults. The manuscript was returned to Rocky Ridge Farm, and Laura began a new project: a story for children about her life in the Big Woods of Wisconsin. This manuscript was accepted by Harper & Brothers and published in April 1932 as *Little House in the Big Woods*.

Laura's stories of her log-cabin life became immediately popular. The Depression years of the 1930s were times of sacrifice for many Americans; Laura's writing reminded people to have courage through hardship.

(opposite, left to right at bottom) This strawberry design decorated the endpapers of Laura's books. It was also used on the cover of the Harper & Brothers 1932 catalogue, which included a description of Little House in the Big Woods, *which received a great deal of publicity when it was first published in 1932. Helen Sewell's picture of Ma and Laura was the frontispiece for* Little House in the Big Woods.

Laura decided to tell the story of Almanzo's boyhood on the farm near Malone, New York. She asked her husband questions, and in his quiet way he responded with stories of his happy boyhood. The resulting book became *Farmer Boy*, published in 1933.

At Rose's suggestion Laura mapped out a whole series of Little House books, to tell the story of the Ingalls and Wilder families all the way to the marriage of Almanzo and Laura. Harper & Brothers was so pleased with the reception of the first two books that it encouraged Laura to continue.

HARPER BOOKS
FOR
BOYS AND GIRLS
1932

HARPER & BROTHERS
49 East 33rd Street, New York

Content material for the eight- to twelve-year-olds is difficult to secure. Here are two volumes which ideally fit this need. One gives a graphic picture of daily life in the Far East. The authors wrote the book to meet the demand encountered through the work of the Child Health Association. . . . Mrs. Wilder's book gives an absorbing picture of frontier life in the Big Woods of Wisconsin, sixty years ago. The experiences of the child in the story are frankly autobiographical.

SPENDING THE DAY
In China, Japan and the Philippines
By SALLY LUCAS JEAN *and* GRACE HALLOCK
Illustrated by JESSIE WILLING *in color and in black and white*
Cloth (6¼ x 8½) (Ages 9-12) $2.00
Simple fact material on how children of other lands live is a recognized need. This book has taken a full day in a typical family in China, Japan and the Philippines. Through this simple method, one sees familiarly the home life, the clothes, the food, the games, the rites and ceremonies, and the average school day. One learns to visualize the homes, outside and in, the streets, the gardens, the market places, and the countryside. One travels as the average small boy and girl in those countries would travel short distances. And through occasionally interpolated stories, one gets a few typical legends and folk tales. Delightful illustrations indicate an artist familiar at first hand with her material. She has succeeded in conveying accurately the facts and at the same time has given something of the colorful background and the atmosphere of the countries depicted.

LITTLE HOUSE IN THE BIG WOODS
By LAURA INGALLS WILDER
Illustrated by HELEN SEWELL *in color and in black and white.*
Cloth (7 x 8½) (Ages 8-12) $2.00

"This little story has a refreshingly genuine and lifelike quality. The author writes of the life she knew and lived sixty years ago on the edge of the Big Woods of Wisconsin. She understands children's tastes and interests and this story is full of incidents and accounts of daily doings that boys and girls will enjoy. Christmas, when visiting aunts, uncles and cousins fill the little house to overflowing; churning and butter-making, hog-killing and 'sugaring-off,' harvest time and pumpkin pies, the wonderful new machine that threshed as much in one day as three men could have threshed in three weeks, and other memories of pioneer life, are described with zest and humor. The characters are very much alive and the portrait of Laura's father, especially, is drawn with loving care and reality."—Anne T. Eaton, N. Y. Times.

10

(top) Pa playing "mad dog" with Laura and Mary in Little House in the Big Woods.

Little House on the Prairie was published in 1935, and this book about the Ingalls family's covered-wagon trip to Kansas became the most popular of all the Little House stories. From all over the world people wrote to Laura expressing pleasure and thanks, and they begged her to continue with her story. Laura was amazed that her books were so loved, and she steadfastly continued to fill her blue-lined tablets with stories.

(top to bottom) Sewell's depiction of Almanzo and his siblings. The Wilder farmhouse today. Almanzo, Royal, and Alice chasing after Lucy the pig.

The money earned by Laura's books meant a small and steady income for Laura and Almanzo. Now in their sixties and seventies, they let their land lie fallow and planted the meadows with grass and clover instead of crops. Almanzo still raised a garden, and he pursued a new hobby: raising a small herd of goats.

On the Banks of Plum Creek was Laura's story of her life near Walnut Grove, Minnesota.

Rocky Ridge Farm,
Mansfield, Missouri,
July 2nd, 1934

Dear Ida Louise Raymond
I am sending you, by express, to-day, the manuscript of my book. Not being able to decide on the title I am enclosing a list of several so you may make the choice.
Like the Little House in the Big Woods and Farmer Boy it is all true and like "The Little House" it is written from my own memories of what happened to us and how we lived, three miles over the line from Kansas, in Indian territory in the years 1870 and 1871.
I do hope you will like the story.
With best regards I am sincerely
Laura Ingalls Wilder

HARPER & BROTHERS
PUBLISHERS
NEW YORK AND LONDON

49 EAST 33RD STREET, NEW YORK, N.Y.

September 11, 1935

My dear Mrs. Wilder:
Here at last are the finished books on LITTLE HOUSE ON THE PRAIRIE, which we are publishing on September 26th. It is a perfectly grand book, and I think that if business conditions improve at all we should repeat the success of LITTLE HOUSE IN THE BIG WOODS. Certainly it is out far enough ahead of Children's Book Week to rate some splendid publicity then. Here's hoping for good sales and good reviews!
Sincerely yours,
Ida Louise Raymond
Department of Books for Boys and Girls

Mrs. Laura Ingalls Wilder
Rocky Ridge Farm
Mansfield, Mo.

ILR/ed

Rocky Ridge Farm
Mansfield, Mo.
Sept. 26, 1935

Dear Miss Raymond,
Your letter of the 11th and the copies of Little House on the Prairie are at hand. They come while I was away from home which explains delay in writing you.
I am glad that you are pleased with the latest Little House and I think myself that with Miss Sewell's illustrations and the make up and all it is a wonderful book. It surely does take Helen Sewell to bring my stories to life.
Please send me three more copies of Little House on the Prairie and charge to my account.
Thanking you for your good wishes I remain sincerely
Laura Ingalls Wilder

As with all of the Little House books, Rose advised Laura, helped her edit her first drafts, and made valuable suggestions. She left Rocky Ridge Farm in 1936 to do research in Columbia, Missouri, so many of her helpful ideas were in the form of letters to Laura. "What you write is always good," Rose wrote her mother.

Rose settled in New York, where she wrote a long magazine serial for *The Saturday Evening Post* entitled "Free Land." She drew on the family past and homesteading for this story, which was a great success when it appeared in 1938. Laura's own story of homesteading in Dakota was titled *By the Shores of Silver Lake*, published in 1939. Mother and daughter conferred about their work and shared information, and each admired what the

(above) Letters went back and forth between Laura and her publisher, Harper & Brothers, during the writing of the series. In the early years Laura's editor was Ida Louise Raymond. (right) Mary and Carrie from Little House on the Prairie.

other wrote. Laura said modestly,
"Rose is a better writer than I
am, but our style of writing
is very similar."

When Rose left Rocky Ridge, Laura and
Almanzo returned to the farmhouse they had built so long ago.
There Laura wrote between preparing meals and baking and housekeeping;
sometimes she woke in the night full of a story that she had to write down.

(above left) Different sketches by Laura's editors for an advertising poster for the fourth Little House book.
(above right) The advertising poster released when On the Banks of Plum Creek *was published in*
1937. (left) Laura in September 1937. This photograph was used to publicize her
trip to a book fair in Detroit, Michigan.
She was 70.

Chapter 22
Storm After Storm

196

The sun shone again in the morning and the winds were still. It seemed much warmer than it really was because the sunshine was so bright.

"It is a beautiful day," Ma said at breakfast, but Pa shook his head. "I don't like it," he said, "The sun is too bright. I'll get a load of hay as soon as I can, for we must have plenty on hand if a storm comes." And he hurried away.

The sun still was shining when Pa came back and after the second meal of the day was eaten, he went across the street for a little while.

When Pa came home, he was whistling cheerfully and carrying a package. "Here is some beef to go with our bread and potatoes. Now we will live like —" he exclaimed as he laid the ... on the table.

"... get beef?" Ma asked.

... his oxen and ... for twenty-five cents ...

At evening still my fancy sees
The flash of snowy wings,
And in my heart
The meadow lark,
Still gaily, sweetly sings.

Laura Ingalls Wilder

By the Author of LITTLE HOUSE IN THE BIG WOODS
BY THE SHORES
of **SILVER LAKE**
LAURA INGALLS WILDER

Drawings by
Helen Sewell and
Mildred Boyle

HARPER & BROTHERS · EST.

Writes Book About Early Settlers Of De Smet Community

MANCHESTER, Nov. 6 — (Special)—"On the Shores of Silver Lake," a new children's book by Laura Ingalls Wilder, was received here last week by relatives of the author.

A story describing the settling of De Smet in 1879 and 1880, the book is one of a series written by Mrs. Wilder, who is a daughter of one of the pioneer residents of the De Smet community, Harper and Brothers are the publishers.

The author and her husband, A. J. Wilder of Mansfield, Mo., were visitors in Manchester and De Smet last June. They are the parents of Rose Wilder Lane, also a noted writer of novels. Mrs. Wilder is at work on another book, a story of the "hard winter" of 1880-81 in the same locality.

In addition to her books, Laura had a heavy correspondence to tend to. She was in steady communication with Rose, with her agent, and with her editor. And Laura answered every fan letter that arrived at Rocky Ridge Farm in her neat, old-fashioned handwriting.

In 1938 Laura and Almanzo took time for a trip west from Rocky Ridge. They invited their friends Neta and Silas Seal to travel with them.

(opposite, near left) Title page and frontispiece for Laura's fourth book. (above, top left) A manuscript page from The Long Winter. *(top right) The first of Laura's five Dakota Territory books, published in 1939. (center left) Laura included her poem of bird life on Silver Lake in copies of the printed book. (bottom right) Grace was a correspondent for the* Huron Daily Plainsman *in 1939, and she submitted this news of her sister's book.*

(left) Almanzo eating his lunch by a creek on the western trip with the Seals in 1938. He liked onion sandwiches because "they make me sleep well." (right) The Wilders with Neta Seal at Yellowstone Park, May 1938. (below) Laura and Almanzo in the Badlands of South Dakota in June 1939.

(bottom left) Mountains, prairies, and the Pacific Ocean were encountered on the 1938 trip, as well as curiosities like an actual house in a tree. (below) Almanzo with his 1936 Chrysler. (opposite) Laura in the Badlands, June 1939.

WORLD FAMOUS TREE HOUSE BELIEVE IT OR NOT

The Seals were much younger; Rose said that her parents regarded them as their children. Together they drove north through California and Oregon, then traveled east again to South Dakota. They stopped in Keystone to see Carrie, who was recently widowed, and then went to Manchester to see Grace and finally to De Smet. There they saw again the prairie of their younger days, the place Laura was writing about in her books. While Laura enjoyed being back on the prairie, she missed Pa and grieved for Ma, who had died in 1924, and Mary, who had died in 1928.

After their return to Mansfield, Laura gave the Seals a copy of one of her books, and in it she wrote:

> *Far over plains and mountains*
> *We traveled once together*
> *And were good friends in every place*
> *In any kind of weather.*
> *Now as you travel life's highway,*
> *This is my thought today,*
> *I wish you a pleasant journey,*
> *And good friends all the way.*

In June 1939 the Wilders were eager to travel once again. Almanzo drove Laura to South Dakota, where they attended De Smet's Old Settlers' Day celebration. They had a fine time visiting old friends, and spending time with Carrie and Grace, and reminiscing.

Laura Ingalls Wilder
BY Anne Harrison

VALENTINE GREETINGS

Laura
To My
Valentine
Ingalls Wilder
Although I've never seen your face.
I feel as though I had.
I've met you in your books, you know,
And they have made me glad.

Anne Mackie

For My Love

Dear Valentine

To My Love

Mad dog

M.L.

Stories

LAURA INGALLS WILDER, THE AUTHOR

L aura's seventh book, *Little Town on the Prairie*, was published in 1941, just before the United States entered World War II. Then came the sad news from South Dakota that Grace had died. Only Laura and Carrie were left in the Little House family.

With wartime restrictions on travel, Laura and Almanzo made no more long trips. They were happy to remain in their little corner of the Ozarks, where they had blessed peace and contentment. Laura's eighth book was published in 1943, when she was seventy-six. It was *These Happy Golden Years*, the story of Laura's teaching, and of her courtship and marriage to Almanzo.

(opposite) Gifts, drawings, letters, and greetings poured in from Laura's readers. (above) Laura picking peas in the garden on Rocky Ridge Farm.

About the Books Themselves

☐ LITTLE HOUSE IN THE BIG WOODS

Over sixty-five years ago, in a log cabin on the edge of the Big Woods of Wisconsin, Mrs. Wilder spent part of her childhood. "This has a refreshingly genuine and life-like quality . . . Christmas, churning and butter-making, hog-killing, and 'sugaring off' are described with zest and humor. The characters are very much alive and the portrait of Laura's father is drawn with loving care and reality." — N. Y. Times. Pictures by Helen Sewell. Ages 8 to 12. Cloth (6¾ x 8½). $2.00.

☐ LITTLE HOUSE ON THE PRAIRIE

The Ingalls family moved from the Big Woods to Kansas, Indian Territory in those days. Some nights there were wolves, often they saw Indians. As always the family made the best of what they had. They planted, plowed, hunted ducks and turkeys, chopped logs. And at the end of a year they were sorry to leave the cabin on the plains for a new land farther west. Pictures by Helen Sewell. Ages 8 to 12. Cloth (6¾ x 8½). $2.00.

☐ FARMER BOY

A year in Almanzo Wilder's boyhood on a big New York state farm over seventy years ago. Almanzo helped with spring planting, with fall threshing, with cutting huge ice blocks and log-hauling in winter. He trained his own team of young twin oxen and won a blue ribbon at the county fair with a giant pumpkin. When spring came again his father gave him Starlight, a beautiful colt, to break in and keep as his own. Pictures by Helen Sewell. Ages 8 to 12. Cloth (6¾ x 8½). $2.00.

☐ ON THE BANKS OF PLUM CREEK

When the Ingalls moved to Minnesota they lived in a sod house until Pa built them a beautiful new one of sweet-smelling wood and real boughten window panes. Laura and Mary loved their new life. Of course there were tragedies — the plague of grasshoppers and the blizzard. But there were good things too, the creek to play in, and in the evenings the sweet music of Pa's fiddle. Pictures by Helen Sewell and Mildred Boyle. Ages 8 to 12. Cloth (6¾ x 8½). $2.00.

☐ BY THE SHORES OF SILVER LAKE

The Ingalls moved next to Dakota Territory in the days of the building of the railroads. Pa was a railroad man until he found a homestead and filed claim. The Ingalls spent the winter in a surveyor's house sixty miles from the nearest neighbor. There was Laura and Mary's thrilling train ride, the attempted payroll robbery, and the Ingalls' happiest Christmas. When spring came Pa put up the first building on the town-site near his claim. And two weeks later there was a brand-new town. Pictures by Helen Sewell and Mildred Boyle. Ages 9 to 13. Cloth (6¼ x 9⅜). $2.00.

☐ THE LONG WINTER

Indian warning said the winter of 1880-81 would be a hard one, so Pa moved his family into town. Blizzards snowed the little town under, cutting off all supplies from the outside. When Christmas had passed and there was a desperate need for food, Almanzo Wilder and another boy made a dangerous trip across the prairie to secure wheat. It was May before the snows melted and the first train got through, bringing the Ingalls' Christmas barrel. Then they had the best and gayest celebration they ever had. Pictures by Helen Sewell and Mildred Boyle. Ages 9 to 13. Cloth (6¼ x 9⅜). $2.00.

☐ LITTLE TOWN ON THE PRAIRIE

Social life soon flourished in the little town — there was a school and a church. Laura went to a wonderful 4th of July celebration, attended her first evening "social"; Almanzo Wilder took her riding behind his dashing team and exchanged the fashionable new "name cards" with her. Things went well with the Ingalls and blind Mary was at last able to go to college. At the very end, when Laura was fifteen, she received her teacher's certificate. Pictures by Helen Sewell and Mildred Boyle. Ages 9 to 13. Cloth (6¼ x 9⅜). $2.00.

☐ THESE HAPPY GOLDEN YEARS

In it Laura teaches her first school, before she is sixteen, in an abandoned claim shanty twelve miles from home. In the summer Mary is home from college, Laura helps the dressmaker in town, and Almanzo breaks colts to drive. There are sleigh rides in winter, buggy rides in summer — and singing school. It is on the way home from singing school one day that Laura and Almanzo become engaged. Then they are married and Laura goes to live with him in another little house on a claim. Ages 10 and up. Cloth (6¼ x 9⅜). $2.00.

Published by

HARPER & BROTHERS

Established 1817

(above) So many readers wrote to Harper & Brothers for information on Laura's books that the publisher issued a brochure listing the titles and giving a biography of the author. (opposite, clockwise from top left) These illustrations for Little Town on the Prairie *reflect how Laura had grown up in the series. A walk down Main Street in De Smet and a party at the depot were part of Laura's rites of passage as she became a young lady in the book. Mansfield, as the Wilders knew it in the 1940s. Laura, Almanzo, and visiting schoolchildren, July 4, 1948.*

Although she was asked to continue the story of her life, Laura decided to retire. She had spent twelve years writing, meeting deadlines, and tending to the business of book making. Her royalties had made life on Rocky Ridge Farm comfortable, and honors and awards assured Laura that she had done valuable work. She was content.

With Almanzo, Laura went riding through the Ozark hills, visiting friends, shopping every Wednesday in Mansfield, and making occasional trips to the larger city of Springfield, fifty miles distant. They attended church dinners and socials and went to the Methodist church on Sundays. Although the townspeople knew that Laura had written books, they had no idea how famous the Wilders were in the world beyond the Ozarks.

In 1944 Carrie paid her last visit to Rocky Ridge

Greetings From Mansfield, Mo.   In The Beautiful Ozark Country

Rocky Ridge Farm
Mansfield, Missouri
April 26, 1943

Dear Miss Nordstrom,

It is great good news that the Little House books will be given first place in the Horn Book.

I will tell you in my rambling way what I think may be useful to Miss Smith and you can choose what you want from it.

Mary graduated from the Iowa College for the Blind in 1889. Her part in an entertainment given by her literary society was an essay entitled "Memory."

You may recollect, in the books I told of Mary's remarkable memory.

In the graduating exercises on June 10th, Mary read another essay, "Bide a Wee and Dinna Weary" which showed the influence of Pa's old Scots songs.

After her graduation Mary lived happily at home with her music, and her raised print and Braile books. She knitted and sewed and took part in the housework.

Pa and Ma and the girls lived for some years in the little house on the homestead, but Pa built a house in the residence part of town and they moved there to be nearer church and

Farm. She was still sprightly and interested in life, and proud of Laura's success as a writer. When Laura and Carrie parted, it was for the last time. Carrie died in 1946, and was buried with the Ingalls family in De Smet.

Laura's books continued to sell so well that her publisher planned to print new editions of them, with illustrations by Garth Williams. Williams traveled to

TO *Laura Ingalls Wilder*

whose contribution to young people's literature has won for her a place among the top 25 . . . writers in the Favorite Author votes of 53,000 mid-west listeners to the radio program, THE HOBBY HORSE PRESENTS, we present this Hobby Horse Favorite Author Award.

THE HOBBY HORSE FAVORITE AUTHOR AWARDS

Ruth Harshaw

Carson Pirie Scott & Company

COMMITTEE

(top left) A letter to editor Ursula Nordstrom at Harper & Brothers about an article in The Horn Book Magazine *paying tribute to Laura and her work. (top right) A group of writers from Topeka, Kansas, visited the Wilders at Rocky Ridge during the summer of 1942. Laura gave them a tour of the farmhouse and served tea, and a discussion of writing was held. A member of the "Scribblers Club" took this photo of Laura and Almanzo.*

most of Laura's old homes to see the locations firsthand, but his most exciting

stop was at Rocky Ridge Farm. He spent the day with Laura and Almanzo,

looking at their old photographs and hearing stories of their lives.

In 1949 Laura and Almanzo were cheered to learn that a library in Detroit was

to be dedicated in Laura's honor. Almanzo was ninety-two and frail, so Laura

could not leave him to appear at the dedication in Michigan. Soon after, he suf-

fered a heart attack, and he died on October 23, 1949, at Rocky Ridge.

Laura's friends and Rose urged her to move to town, or have someone live at

Rocky Ridge. Laura accepted neither suggestion. "I do not mind living alone,"

she said firmly, "except for missing Almanzo. I am very lonely for him, but that

would be so

wherever I was."

(opposite, center) A mailing envelope from Laura's publishers. Almost all Laura's correspondence with her editors was by mail or telegram. (opposite, bottom) Listeners of "The Hobby Horse," a radio program in Chicago, elected Laura their favorite author in 1947. A birthday party for Laura was held on the air for her 80th birthday. (right) Garth Williams' 1947 photo of the Ingalls homestead land near De Smet. (far right) Laura faith-fully sent donations to the De Smet Cemetery to keep the Ingalls family graves well tended.

Laura's nine Little House books, with new covers and illustrations by Garth Williams. The First Four Years was published after Laura's death, in 1971.

1950 1957

THE LITTLE HOUSE LEGACY

During the 1950s the Little House books and their author received honors and recognitions from far and wide. The books were considered by many to be classics, and were among the most popular books for children in America. A library room was named for Laura in 1950 in far-off Pomona, California, and the next year Mansfield dedicated its library to her. Laura's books and their influence extended worldwide, with translations into German, Japanese, Chinese, and other languages.

(above) Laura and her driver, Jim Harley, and her new 1954 green Oldsmobile.

(right) A deer in the Big Woods, one of Williams' first Little House illustrations.

69

St. Louis Globe-Democrat
TUESDAY MORNING, JULY 4, 1950

Features

SECTION D

PAGES 1 TO 16

Ozark Woman Started With Tablet and Pencil and Went On to Become a Famous Novelist

Mansfield, Mo.
October 8th 1951

Dear Miss Nordstrom,

I have thought that perhaps you and others of your office might like to have one of the bookmarks that were given to guests at the open house which followed dedecation of the library ~~no~~ here, now offically the "Laura Ingalls Wilder Library"

Fortunately I was able to be there and the affair was very enjoyable.

Kindest regards to you and others of your office

Laura Ingalls Wilder

The Laura Ingalls Wilder Library

By Appreciation We Make Excellence In Others Our Own Property

~ Voltaire

Laura's mail remained heavy as her admirers increased, and she was constantly busy acknowledging the heartfelt letters that came to her. Her eighty-fourth birthday in 1951 brought nearly a thousand greetings. Her readers came visiting, finding the way to Rocky Ridge in hopes of a word with Laura or a glimpse of her at home. Often, Laura invited her new friends in for a tour of the old farmhouse.

Rose came for visits from her home in Danbury, Connecticut, and once Laura surprised everyone by returning with Rose for a visit—by airplane. It was Laura's first plane ride. How times had changed since her first train ride and her many trips by covered wagon!

(above) Rose's house in Danbury, Connecticut.

(opposite, clockwise from top): A headline in the St. Louis Globe-Democrat, *published on July 4, 1950. Laura in 1954. A bookmark given out at the dedication of Mansfield's Laura Ingalls Wilder Library. A letter to Laura's editor, Ursula Nordstrom.*

In 1953, after six years of planning, Harper & Brothers published the new editions of all eight Little House books with hundreds of carefully researched illustrations by Garth Williams. Laura was pleased with the books and amazed that her stories of pioneer times grew steadily in fame and in importance all over the world. "I am glad if my books have helped," she remarked modestly when she was told that children learned valuable American history through the Little House stories.

THE HORN BOOK
MAGAZINE
December, 1953

ILLUSTRATING
THE LITTLE HOUSE BOOKS
By GARTH WILLIAMS

WHEN Ursula Nordstrom asked me to illustrate the new edition of the Laura Ingalls Wilder books I wanted very much to do so. I loved and admired the books myself and they had meant a great deal to my small daughters when we read them aloud together. But my knowledge of the West at that time was almost zero and I could not see myself undertaking the work happily until I had seen the country that formed the background of the stories. And so I decided to visit Mrs. Wilder in Mansfield, Missouri, where she still lives; and then follow the route which the Ingalls family took in their covered wagon.

I was spending the summer with my family on a very primitive farm in New York State. We had neither telephone nor electricity. The house had five barns and a smokehouse. Our water came down from a crystal-clear spring in the woods, and our only mechanical convenience was a hand-pump in the kitchen, located in a lean-to with a very leaky roof. We were situated on a high hill surrounded by two hundred acres. The house was almost two hundred years old and the main barn was 413

NOW—to be cherished forever—
in a beautiful new edition . . .
The eight "Little House" books of

Laura Ingalls Wilder

with superb new illustrations
by Garth Williams

(clockwise from top) Ma and Laura making cheese in Little House in the Big Woods. Harper & Brothers' publicity brochure announcing the new editions of the Little House books. In 1953 The Horn Book Magazine paid tribute to Laura Ingalls Wilder and commemorated the publication of new editions of the Little House books with illustrations by Garth Williams.

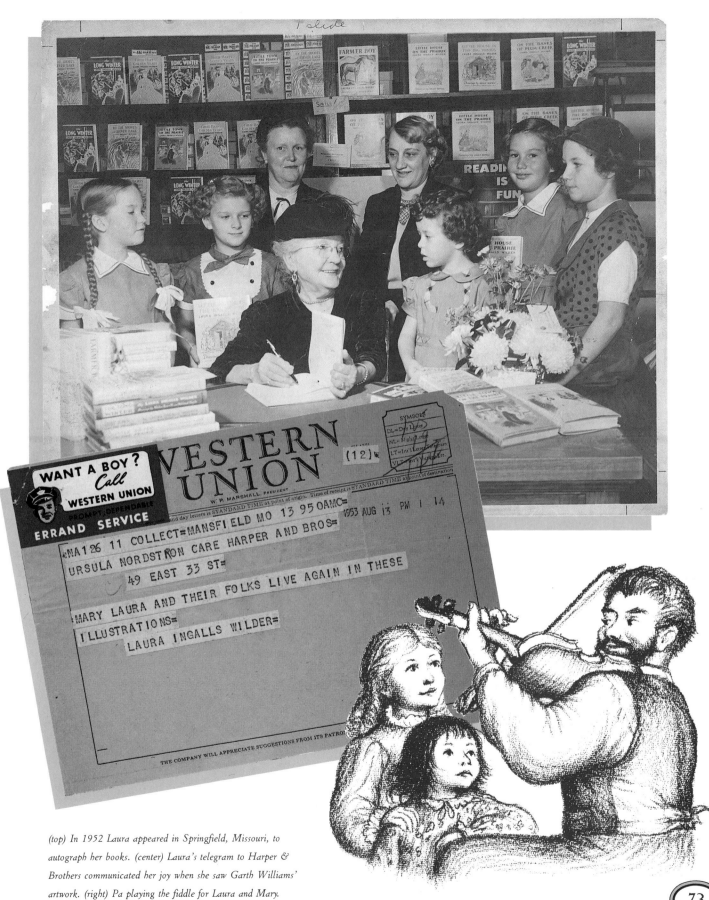

(top) In 1952 Laura appeared in Springfield, Missouri, to autograph her books. (center) Laura's telegram to Harper & Brothers communicated her joy when she saw Garth Williams' artwork. (right) Pa playing the fiddle for Laura and Mary.

Laura's last years were quiet ones; increasingly, she stayed close to Rocky Ridge Farm. She read stacks of books from the Laura Ingalls Wilder Library in Mansfield; she pored over piles of mail from her readers all over the world; she welcomed the visits of friends and neighbors who kindly looked in on her.

At the beginning of 1957 Laura was eighty-nine, soon to be ninety. She wanted to reach ninety, she said, because Almanzo had. All over America celebrations were planned for Laura's birthday. Cards and gifts were delivered to Rocky Ridge in time for Laura's ninetieth birthday on February seventh. Laura and Rose, who was visiting, were amazed by the piles of birthday greetings.

WESTERN UNION

W. P. MARSHALL, PRESIDENT

CLASS OF SERVICE

This is a full-rate
Telegram or Cable-
gram unless its de-
ferred character is in-
dicated by a suitable
symbol above or pre-
ceding the address.

SYMBOLS

DL = Day Letter
NL = Night Letter
LT = Int'l Letter Telegram
VLT = Int'l Victory Ltr.

The filing time shown in the date line on telegrams and day letters is STANDARD TIME at point of origin. Time of receipt is STANDARD TIME at point of destination

K CK NL PD   SAGNANAW MICH FEB 6TH 57

MRS LAURA INGALLS WILDER
ROCKY RIDGE FARM
MANSFIELD MO...

DEAR LAURA . ON YOUR NINETIETH BIRTHDAY THE BOYS AND GIRLS THEIR
TEACHERS AND LIBRARIANS SEND HAPPY BIRTHDAY WISHES . EACH OF US
SEND A GREETING ALTHOUGH FIFTEEN THOUSAND OF US CANNOT SIGN THIS
MESSAGE . WE WISH YOU COULD COME TO THE GINGERBREAD PARTY AT THE
PUBLIC LIBARY . WITH LOVE AND BEST WISHES . FOR YOUR HAPPINESS .

YOUR FRIENDS IN SAGINAW MICH.

713 A

THE COMPANY WILL APPRECIATE SUGGESTIONS FROM ITS PATRONS CONCERNING ITS SE

In Honor Of
Laura Ingalls Wilder
Noted Children's Author
Wright County Library
Invites You To Send Her
Birthday Greetings
February 7 Mansfield Missouri

*(opposite, top) Laura and Neta Seal at Rocky Ridge Farm. (above, left and opposite) Birthday cards and greetings from a school in Saginaw,
Michigan, and elsewhere. (top) Laura in one of her favorite dresses. (bottom, right) Laura at a party held in her honor.*

July, 30th 1952

Rose Dearest,

When you read this I will be gone and you will have inherited all I have.

Please give to the Laura Ingalls Wilder Library in Mansfield all that is left in my private library after you have taken from it want you want for yourself. This includes the framed testimonials from Chicago, California and the Pacific North West.

My jewelry is unique and should not be carelessly scattered. Do with it as you wish but preserve it in some way if you can.

We were proud of my Havalind china but loved best the English made blue Willow ware. Do as you please with all the china, but I wish you might use it.

The persimon-wood chair and the cypress stand-table that Manly made belong to Silas Seal.

My love will be with you always
Mama Bess
(Laura Ingalls Wilder)

Then, three days later, Laura died. On February 10, 1957, Laura the pioneer girl, Laura the farmer's wife, and Laura the author was gone. But her pioneering spirit is remembered, more so each year, and her stories, which open the door to the past, will live on for generations to come.

(above) At 85, Laura wrote her wishes to Rose, in a letter to be opened upon her death.
(opposite) Laura on Rocky Ridge Farm, March 1954; she was 87.

"Spring has come to the Ozarks. The hills are green with new grass, buds are swelling on the trees, spring flowers are blooming. . . ."

"These years are very pleasant, with good friends and kind neighbors. . . ."

"The only way to go is ahead. . . ."

A LAURA INGALLS WILDER CHRONOLOGY

1807   Henry Newton Quiner born.

1809   Charlotte Wallis Tucker born.

1810   Laura Colby born.

1812   Lansford Whiting Ingalls born.

1836   January 10
Charles Phillip Ingalls born in Cuba,
New York.

1839   December 12
Caroline Lake Quiner born in Milwaukee
County, Wisconsin.

1857   February 13
Almanzo James Wilder born near
Malone, New York.

1860   February 1
Charles Ingalls and Caroline Quiner
marry in Concord, Wisconsin.

1863   September 23
Charles Ingalls purchases Pepin farm.

1865   January 10
Mary Amelia Ingalls born in Pepin,
Wisconsin.

1867   February 7
Laura Elizabeth Ingalls born in Pepin.

1870   August 3
Caroline Celestia (Carrie) Ingalls born in
Montgomery County, Kansas.

1871   The Ingalls family return to the
Pepin farm.

1874   The Ingalls family move to Walnut
Grove, Minnesota.

1875   November 1
Charles Frederick Ingalls born in Walnut
Grove.

1876   August 27
Charles Frederick Ingalls dies; buried in
South Troy, Minnesota.

1876–1877   The Ingalls family live in
Burr Oak, Iowa.

1877   May 23
Grace Pearl Ingalls born in Burr Oak.

1878–1879   The Ingalls family live in
Walnut Grove.

1879   The Ingalls family move to Dakota
Territory.

1885   August 25
Laura Ingalls and Almanzo Wilder
marry in De Smet, Dakota Territory.

1886   December 5
Rose Wilder born in De Smet.

1889   August
Laura and Almanzo's son is born and
dies in De Smet.

1891–1892   The Wilders visit Florida.

1894   Laura, Almanzo, and Rose Wilder
settle in Mansfield, Missouri.